To Terry Cranley

Contents

MISSISSIPPI MUD

William Gillock

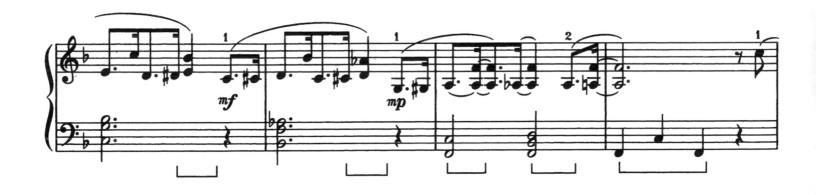

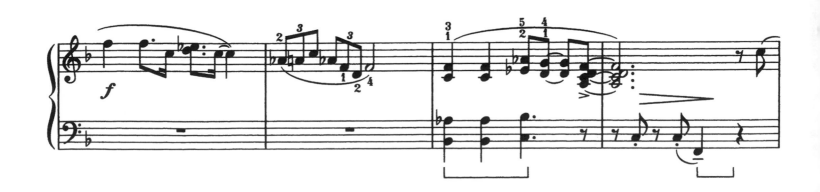

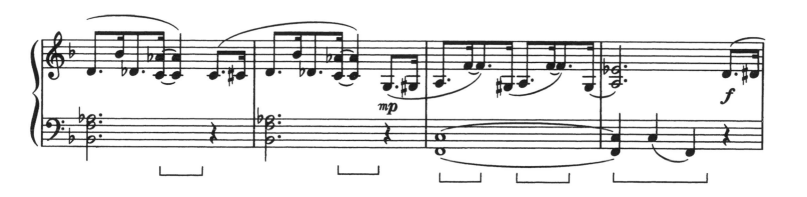

UPTOWN BLUES

William Gillock

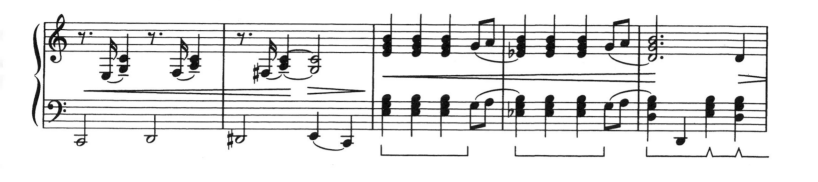

DOWNTOWN BEAT

William Gillock

CANAL STREET BLUES

William Gillock

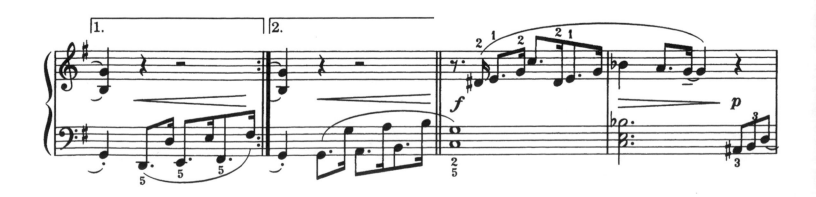

BILL BAILEY

32/33

WON'T YOU PLEASE COME HOME

Hughie Canon
Arranged by William Gillock

light staccato throughout, like a plucked string bass